Contenido del CD:

(duración total: 24'15")

Introducción
1. Introducción musical

Diálogos con ambientación sonora

2. Págs. 2-3
3. Págs. 4-5
4. Págs. 6-7
5. Págs. 8-9
6. Págs. 10-11
7. Págs. 12-13
8. Págs. 14-15

9. Págs. 16-17
10. Págs. 18-19
11. Págs. 20-21
12. Págs. 22-23
13. Págs. 24-25
14. Págs. 26-27
15. Págs. 28-29

Diálogos (versión lenta para repetir)

16. Págs. 2-3
17. Págs. 4-5
18. Págs. 6-7
19. Págs. 8-9
20. Págs. 10-11
21. Págs. 12-13
22. Págs. 14-15

23. Págs. 16-17
24. Págs. 18-19
25. Págs. 20-21
26. Págs. 22-23
27. Págs. 24-25
28. Págs. 26-27
29. Págs. 28-29

Vocabulario
30. Vocabulario inglés-español
31. Vocabulario inglés (versión lenta para repetir)

> **Nota para padres y educadores:**
> Para facilitar la identificación de las locuciones con los diálogos, cada personaje se representa con una letra inicial: C (Cat), M (Mouse), W (Waiter) y P (cricket Player).

Título original: *J'apprends l'anglais avec Cat and Mouse - Go to London!*
© ABC MELODY Editions, 2015
All rights reserved throughout the world.
© Grupo Anaya, S.A., Madrid, 2015
Juan Ignacio Luca de Tena, 15. 28027 Madrid
www.anayainfantilyjuvenil.com

1.ª edición: febrero de 2015
3.ª edición: julio de 2018

Dirección artística, música y producción: Stéphane Husar
Ilustraciones: Loïc Méhée
Locución: Brian Scott Bagley y Juan Megías Soriano

ISBN: 978-84-678-7101-2
Depósito legal: M-262-2015
Impreso en España - Printed in Spain

Aprendo inglés con

Cat and Mouse
Go to London!

Stéphane Husar – Loïc Méhée

ANAYA

It is 7 o'clock.
Mouse is sleeping.
Cat runs into the bedroom.

C: Wake up, Mouse!
It's a beautiful day.
M: Go away, Cat! I'm sleeping.
C: Get up! I've got a great idea.
Let's go to London!
M: Let's have breakfast first!
C: We can have breakfast
in London.
Come on, Mouse!

3

M: I'm hungry.

C: Smile, Mouse!

M: What are you doing?

C: I'm taking a selfie. Smile!

M: Hurry up, Cat! Get in the car!

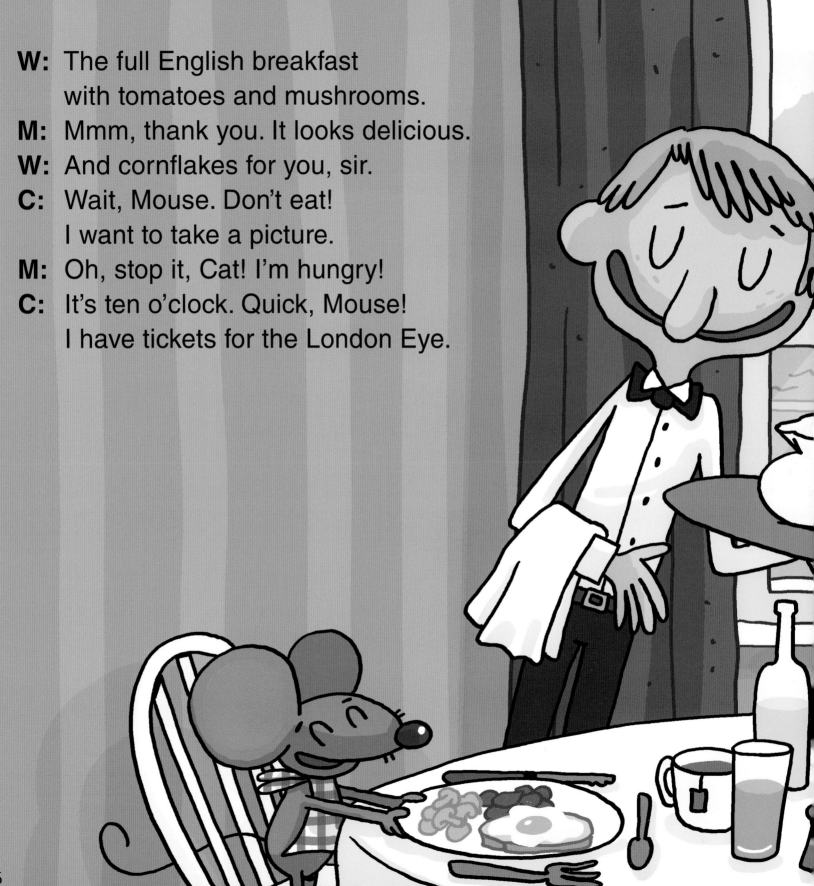

W: The full English breakfast
with tomatoes and mushrooms.

M: Mmm, thank you. It looks delicious.

W: And cornflakes for you, sir.

C: Wait, Mouse. Don't eat!
I want to take a picture.

M: Oh, stop it, Cat! I'm hungry!

C: It's ten o'clock. Quick, Mouse!
I have tickets for the London Eye.

C: Look, Mouse! You can see all of London.

M: Wow, it's beautiful!

C: Come here, Mouse! Let's take a selfie with Big Ben.

M: Take one with Buckingham Palace, too.

C: We'll go there next.

M: Is that Buckingham Palace?
C: Yes, it is. Look, the Queen is here.
M: Where? I don't see the Queen!

C: She's in the Palace.
M: How do you know?
C: Look up there!
The Royal Standard is flying.

M: Do you see a restaurant, Cat? I'm hungry!

C: You can't be hungry, Mouse!
Let's stand in front of that phone box.
I'll take a picture.
Now, let's sit next to that postbox.

M: Now, let's have lunch, Cat!

13

M: Yum! Fish and Chips! Let's get takeaway, Cat!

C: Good idea, Mouse! We can go to Hyde Park for a picnic.

M: Hurry, Cat! Here's the bus for Hyde Park.

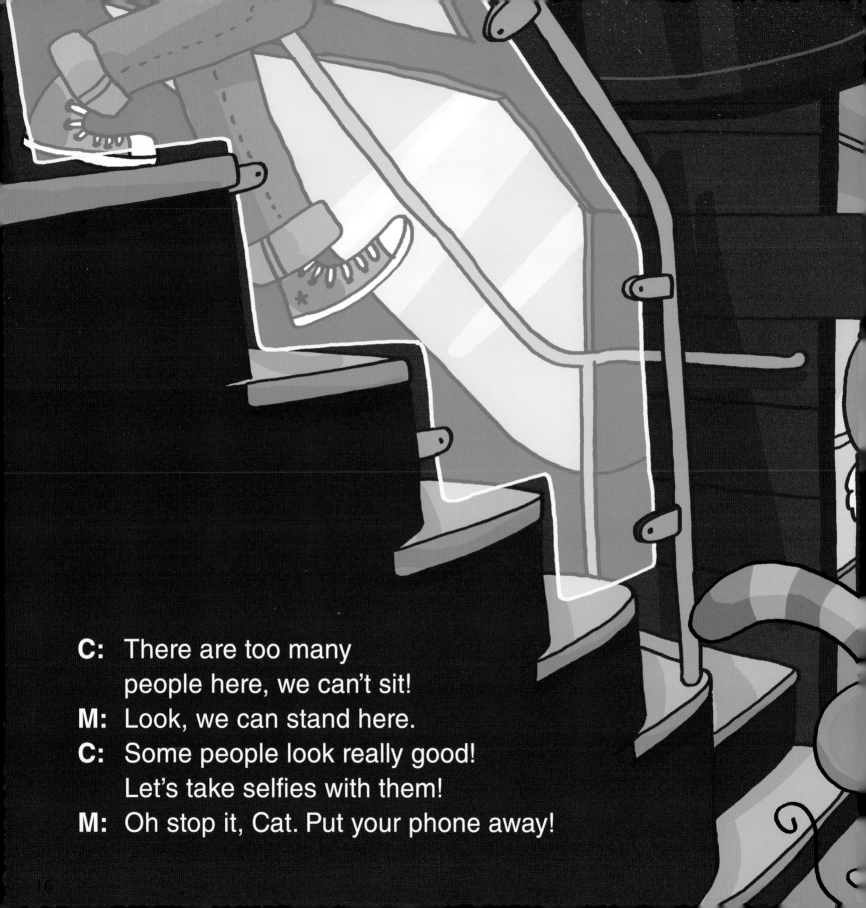

C: There are too many
people here, we can't sit!

M: Look, we can stand here.

C: Some people look really good!
Let's take selfies with them!

M: Oh stop it, Cat. Put your phone away!

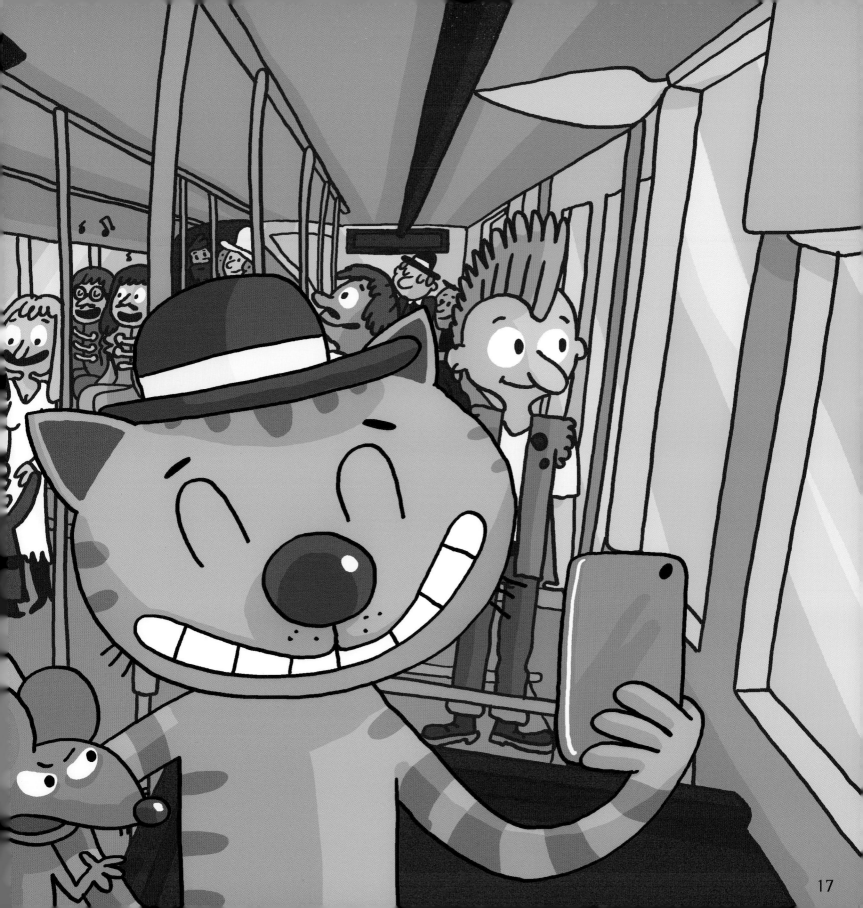

M: This is a big park!
C: There's a lot to do here.
M: You can go for a walk.
C: You can cycle.
M: You can rollerblade.
C: You can play tennis.

M: You can row a boat.
   Hey! What are you doing? Sit down, Cat!
C: I'm taking a selfie...
M: Hee! Hee! You can swim at Hyde Park.

C: Oh!

M: What's that, Cat?

C: It's a cricket ball. Miaow!

M: Do you like to play cricket?

C: I love to play cricket!
I'm a great cricket player.

P: Do you want to play with us?

C: Wait! Let's take a selfie first…

M: Stop it Cat. Come on, let's go and play!

M: Are you OK, Cat?

C: No, I'm not! Stupid game, my head hurts!

M: Here, have a biscuit.

C: Oh! What are you doing, Mouse?

M: I'm taking a selfie. Smile!

C: Arrrgh! I want to go home!

M: I want to buy a souvenir.
I want to go to Hamleys. Let's go, Cat!

M: This is a big toy shop.
C: Hamleys is the biggest toy shop in the world!
M: Look at this teddy bear. It's big.
C: Wow, it's the biggest teddy bear in the world!
M: Do you like it?
C: I love it. Let's buy it! Miaow!

25

C: I love London!

M: Me too! Give me your phone, Cat.

C: What are you doing, Mouse?

M: I'm making a photo album. Look!

Vocabulario inglés-español de Cat and Mouse

Wake up!: ¡Despierta!

Get up!: ¡Levanta!

Go away!: ¡Vete!

Let's go to London!: ¡Vamos a Londres!

Let's have breakfast!: ¡Vamos a desayunar!

What are you doing?: ¿Qué estás haciendo?

I'm taking a *selfie*: Estoy haciendo un *selfie* (una autofoto).

It's ten o'clock: Son las diez en punto.

The Queen is here: La reina está aquí.

Let's get takeaway!: Pidamos comida para llevar.

Hurry / hurry up!: ¡Deprisa! / ¡Rápido!

Put your phone away!: ¡Guarda tu móvil!

There's a lot to do here: Hay un montón de cosas que hacer aquí.

Do you like to play cricket?: ¿Te gusta jugar al críquet?

I want to buy a *souvenir*: Quiero comprar un recuerdo.